Corey's Dad Drinks Too Much

Anne Courtney
Illustrated by Melodye Rosales

An Eager Reader
Tyndale House Publishers, Inc.
Wheaton, Illinois

Library of Congress Cataloging-in-Publication Data

Courtney, Anne, date
    Corey's dad drinks too much / Anne Courtney ; illustrated by
Melodye Rosales.
        p.   cm.
    Summary: Uses a Christian perspective to discuss alcoholism in a
parent and how it can be treated.
    ISBN 0-8423-0223-9
    1. Children of alcoholics—Juvenile literature.   2. Alcoholics—
Rehabilitation—Juvenile literature.   3. Alcoholism—Religious
aspects—Christianity—Juvenile literature.   [1. Alcoholism.]
I. Rosales, Melodye, ill.   II. Title.
HV5132.C69   1991
362.29'23—dc20   91-65135

Ask your bookstore for other Eager Reader books:
Alfred MacDuff Is Afraid of War
Stranger Danger
Natalie Jean and the Flying Maching
Natalie Jean Goes Hog Wild
Natalie Jean and Tag-along Tessa
Natalie Jean and the Haints' Parade

The Scripture quotation on page 40 is from The Simplified Living Bible
© 1990 by KNT Charitable Trust. All rights reserved.

98 97 96 95 94 93 92 91
 9   8   7   6   5   4   3   2   1

Contents

One

Dad Drinks
Too Much

Hi! I'm Corey.

I wish my dad wouldn't drink. I used to think it was OK. Other grown-ups drink. But Dad drinks *a lot*. He never has just one.

After work he pops open a can of beer. He watches TV. He reads the newspaper. He opens another can of beer. And then another.

I showed him the kite I made. He didn't even look.

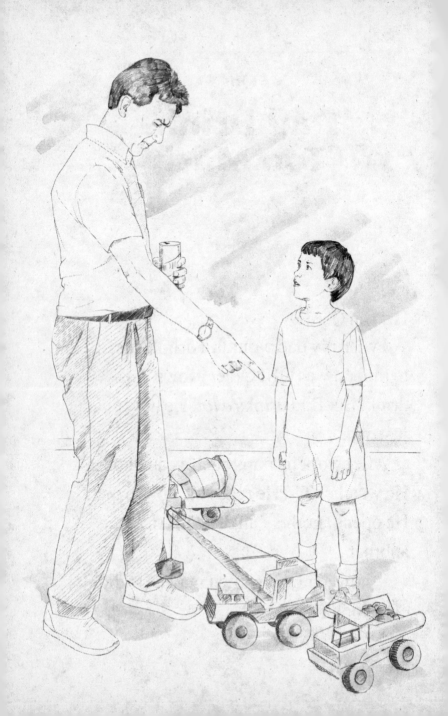

Why can't you hear me, Dad?
Why can't you stop drinking?

When Dad drinks, he acts different. He talks funny. He walks crooked. That's drunk.

When he drinks, he gets mad. I forgot to pick up my cars and he tripped. He yelled at me.

I didn't mean to forget. I didn't like his loud voice.

Dad, if I always remember to pick up my toys, then will you stop drinking?

Two

Two Kinds of Dads

Dad is nice when he doesn't drink.

He helps me with my schoolwork. He taught me to ride my bike. He took me to a baseball game. He even got me a puppy named Toby.

But when he drinks, he isn't so nice.

He yells at Mom. They argue. Once he broke her pretty vase. She cried. I was scared. I thought Dad might hurt Mom.

I feel mixed up. There are two dads at my house—the nice one and the one who drinks and acts mean.

Dad, I don't like you when you drink.
I want to throw your beer away.

11

Dad promised to come to my soccer game. He didn't.

He said we'd go to a movie. He came home late.

I felt disappointed and mad again.

I want my friends to come over, but what if Dad drinks? I'll be embarrassed.

Other dads don't drink too much. Why can't you be like them?

Three

God Cares

I play in my room with Toby.

He's my friend. I like to talk to him.
He's soft and warm. He makes me smile.

But I still feel sad and lonely when Dad
drinks.

*Please stop drinking, Dad! For
me—and Mom—and you, too.*

I wonder if God sees me when I'm in my room. Does He know I'm afraid when Dad and Mom argue? Does He know I'm sad?

Yes, God knows everything. He knows
all about me. He knows where I live. He
knows when I'm happy or sad or scared.
He knows about Dad, too.

I feel good about knowing God is always with me. He never leaves me. I can talk to Him like I talk to Toby.

God is my friend. I feel better when I talk to Him. The Bible says that God loves me. He cares for me.

Dad, I know God cares for you, too.

Four
Dad Is Sick

When Dad drinks, Mom acts different. She's kind of sad. I see her crying.

She worries when Dad's late from work. Sometimes she's so worried she doesn't pay attention to me.

She gets mad and yells, even when it's not my fault. She even yells at Toby.

One day Mom went to a special meeting. It was called Al-Anon. She met other people there who have someone in their family who drinks a lot.

Now she goes to meetings every week.
She smiles more and doesn't cry as much.
She doesn't get so mad. I like that!

Mom says Dad can't stop drinking by himself. He needs help.

He has a sickness called alcoholism. It isn't like chicken pox or a cold or the flu. Alcohol makes some people sick.

Alcohol makes Dad sick. It makes him act different, too. He says and does things he doesn't mean.

One drink makes him want more.

And more.

And more.

Dad, you don't look sick. You don't have spots. You're not in bed.

Alcoholism is hard to understand.

A lot of people have this sickness. Moms can have it, not just dads.

Mom told me it's not my fault Dad drinks. He would still drink even if I always got good grades . . . or tried to be really good . . . or remembered to pick up my toys. Something in his body makes him want alcohol.

He isn't a bad dad. He's a sick dad.

Dad, I'm sorry you're sick.

I want you to get better.

Five
Dad Can Get Better

Something else I learned about alcoholism is that people can get well. Dad can, too!

But it is really hard. He will need lots of help. He will have to stop drinking alcohol forever.

Dad needs God's help most of all. He needs to ask God to help him stop drinking. The Bible says God gives us strength to do all kinds of hard things.

Dad, I know God will help you if you ask Him.

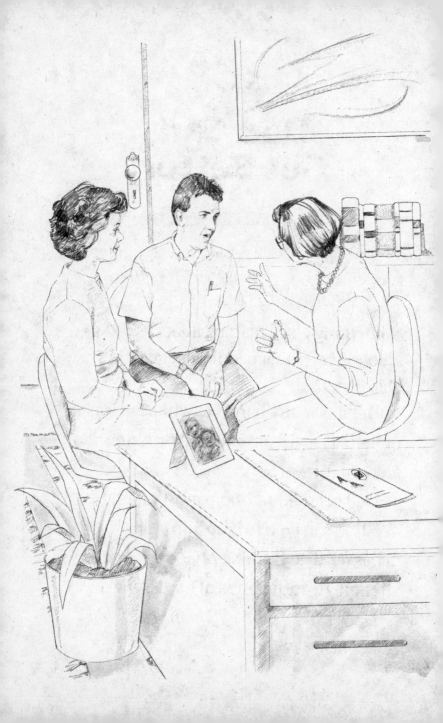

Sometimes people who have this sickness don't think they need help. They blame everyone else.

Mom says a counselor can help us plan a special meeting with Dad. We'll tell him how much we love him. I can tell him how I feel when he drinks: sad, lonely, embarrassed, mad, confused, afraid. The counselor will tell Dad how he can get well.

Hospitals for people who have alcoholism are called treatment centers. Dad can go to one of them to start getting better.

Dad will need other people to help him, too. He can go to meetings called A.A. (Alcoholics Anonymous). People who want to stop drinking go there.

They talk about what it was like when they were drinking. They tell how happy they are not to be drinking now. They thank God for helping them.

Six

I Feel Better, Too

It takes a long time to get better.

Everything won't be OK just because Dad stops drinking. But things will be better.

Mom says Dad's sickness has hurt all of us. It will take time for us to feel better, too.

Some things I can do to feel better:

- I can remember Dad is an alcoholic. I can be patient with him because he's sick.

- I can talk about my feelings. I can talk to:

God	Toby	Grandpa
Pastor	Mom	Grandma
Friends		Counselors

- I can know it's not my fault Dad drinks. I didn't make him start drinking. I can't make him stop drinking.

- Dad says and does things he doesn't mean when he drinks. I can forgive him.

- People who have alcoholism can get well. I can pray for Dad.

Dad, I love you.
I don't like your sickness, but I love you.
I will keep praying for you to get better.

Seven

Prayer

Dear God,

It's hard to understand why Dad can't stop drinking. It's hard to understand alcoholism, but I'm trying.

I'm glad You can help people get well. Please help Dad get better.

Thank You for helping me when it's hard—especially when I'm sad or afraid.

Thank You for my family. Thank You for Dad and the nice things he does. Thank You for Mom.

I love You, God. I'm glad You're my friend. Thank You for loving me and my family.

Amen.

Let God have all your worries and cares. He is always thinking about you and watching everything that concerns you.

(1 Peter 5:7)

Suggestions for Parents

1. Learn about alcoholism. Identifying the problem and becoming informed is the first step toward recovery.

The following organizations provide information:

National Council on Alcoholism
    12 West Twenty-first Street
    New York, NY 10010

For alcoholics:
    Alcoholics Anonymous
    P.O. Box 459, Grand Central Station
    New York, NY 10163
    (local offices listed in the telephone book)

For family members of alcoholics:
    Al-Anon or Alateen

P.O. Box 862, Midtown Station
    New York, NY 10018-0862
    (local offices listed in the telephone book)

For Christian alcoholics:
>   Alcoholics Victorious
>   P.O. Box 10364
>   Portland, OR 97210
>   (503) 245-9629

For Christians struggling with
>   *addictions/dysfunctional families:*
>   Overcomers Outreach
>   2290 W. Whittier Blvd., Suite D
>   La Habra, CA 90631
>   (213) 697-3994

>   Treatment centers
>   (listed in yellow pages of the telephone book)

2. Become involved in a support group. Your child will benefit from the help you receive. Contact Al-Anon. One of its local offices can provide a schedule of meetings in your area. Or contact churches. Many of them offer Christ-centered programs.

3. Communicate openly with your child. Explain the disease and what is happening. Children have an amazing ability to deal with the truth.

4. Reassure your child that he or she is loved and isn't responsible for a parent's drinking.

5. Show compassion for the alcoholic family member. Children learn by example. They won't be forced to take sides if you are compassionate.

6. Examine your attitudes. Be willing to admit when you're wrong and ask for forgiveness.

7. Treat your child with courtesy and consideration. Be tolerant of mistakes.

8. Encourage the honest expression of emotions. Let your child know it's OK to talk about feelings— negative as well as positive. Be willing to listen without criticism.

9. Provide a stable environment. As much as possible, adhere to a familiar schedule. Be consistent in maintaining limits. This gives children a sense of security.

10. Refuse to tolerate unacceptable behavior. Your child will sense your strength and not be so frightened if volatile situations are avoided.

Living with alcoholism is difficult, but with God's help, families recover. The long chain of effects from alcoholism, passed down through generations, can be broken.

God bless you!